Oscar Wilde's

An Ideal Husband
Companion

*Includes Study Guide, Historical Context,
Biography, and Character Index*

BookCaps™ Study Guides

www.bookcaps.com

© 2013. All Rights Reserved.

Table of Contents

Historical Context

Oscar Wilde was born in 1854 in Dublin, Ireland. His successful parents combined with natural writing genius earned him numerous awards and scholarships throughout his youth. He went to college at both Trinity and Oxford, where he honed his writing skills and also helped found the aesthetic movement.

After his time in school, he moved to London, England, where he became what some call the original "dandy". A dandy is a man who is young, overly concerned with appearance, intellectual and rebellious. Many of Oscar Wilde's characters exemplify these characteristics, and sometimes serve to represent Oscar Wilde himself. Lord Goring in An Ideal Husband, for instance, is an example of this.

The early 1890's brought Oscar Wilde to the height of his career. His novel, Dorian Gray, first earned him fame through its scandalous exploration of Victorian themes. Shortly after the novel Dorian Gray, Oscar Wilde began producing plays. An Ideal Husband was written in 1893, after Dorian Gray and before The Importance of Being Earnest.

He began writing An Ideal Husband during the summer of 1893, and completed it that same winter. The first theatre he sent the manuscript to refused it, but the Haymarket theatre decided to put it on. The Haymarket had been taken over by a man named Lewis Waller, and wasn't doing too well. Waller, also a talented actor, played Robert Chiltern in the original run. The huge success of the play brought Oscar Wilde into the forefront of theatre, and that same year he released The Importance of Being Earnest, his most successful play.

Soon after his plays opened on the stage, however, Oscar's name was taken off them because of his arrest. In the early 1890's, no one is sure exactly when, Oscar Wilde began having an affair with Lord Alfred Douglas. It was this affair that led to his arrest, and because of the sensitivity to homosexuality in society at the time, no one wanted his name associated with the plays any longer. When the manuscript for An Ideal Husband was eventually published in 1899, Oscar Wilde's name still did not appear as the author.

Looking back at the events of Oscar's life at the time, it is easy to see how Oscar Wilde inserts himself and his personal experiences into his plays. Oscar was blackmailed by a friend who found a love letter to Alfred just as Robert was blackmailed by Mrs. Cheveley with a letter from his past. Oscar rebelled against the norms of Victorian society and urged forgiveness for sins instead of judgment. In this respect, Oscar also resembles Sir Robert.

Oscar Wilde's firm belief in aestheticism also comes across strongly in his plays, especially his dandy characters such as Lord Goring. Aestheticism is a philosophy which upholds beauty, freedom and style above other, more constricting, morals common in that era of society. Up until his arrest, Oscar lived a relatively carefree life. He floated around in fashionable circles, enjoyed talking about philosophy extensively, and, in general, lived for pleasure. This is why characters such as Lord Caversham are seen as stuffy and unpleasant, while characters such as Lord Goring are oddly admirable.

Plot Summary

The first scene opens on a dinner party being hosted by Sir Robert Chiltern and his wife, Lady Chiltern, in the fashionable part of London. Sir Robert is a well-to-do politician and a member of the House of Commons and Lady Chiltern is his virtuous, beautiful wife. Several guests, all members of high society, are there, including Mrs. Marchmont, Lady Basildon, and the Vicomte De Nanjac. Lord Caversham and his son, Lord Goring, a bachelor and dandy, are also present.

During the party, one of Lady Chiltern's older friends, Mrs. Markby, comes in with her guest, Mrs. Cheveley. Lady Chiltern immediately recognizes Mrs. Cheveley as one of her old schoolmates with a cruel, deceitful temperament. Lady Chiltern knows Mrs. Cheveley is up to no good, and soon Mrs. Cheveley shows her true colors by blackmailing Sir Robert Chiltern. She has in her possession a letter from Robert's past proving that he sold Cabinet secrets to the Baron Arnheim in his youth. Mrs. Cheveley demands that Robert support a canal project she is invested in at his next meeting. The project is a scam, and Robert refuses to support it, but is forced to because of the letter.

After getting Robert's word, Mrs. Cheveley talks to Lady Chiltern. She reveals that Robert agreed to support her, and Lady Chiltern is angry. Lady Chiltern worships her husband and believes him to be above all other men in matters of honor.

The last two guests remaining at the party are Mabel Chiltern, Robert's sister, and Lord Goring. Conversing on a couch, Mabel finds a diamond brooch. Lord Goring takes the brooch from her, saying he gave it to someone as a present. He also wants Mabel to tell him if anyone comes to claim it. Lord Goring and Mabel soon leave, as well.

When Robert and Lady Chiltern are alone, she pleads with him not to go through with it. Not aware of her husband's past or the letter, she vows to never see him again if he has a shameful past. Assuring her he does not, he agrees to write Mrs. Cheveley a letter declining her proposal. By doing so, he seals his political and personal doom.

The second act also takes place at Robert's house but in the drawing room. Lord Goring is waiting for Robert, who finally appears. Robert is distressed about the situation and asks Lord Goring for advice. Lord Goring, having been shortly engaged to Mrs. Cheveley before finding out her dishonest nature, has some insight. He advises Robert to tell Lady Chiltern the situation and to fight Mrs. Cheveley any way he can. Robert won't tell Lady Chiltern because he will risk losing her, but agrees something must be done. Mabel comes in, and she and Lord Goring engage in witty, flirty conversation. During his visit, Lord Goring also urges Lady Chiltern to be more forgiving of other's offenses.

When Lord Goring leaves, Mrs. Markby comes by with Mrs. Cheveley, who is inquiring about her missing brooch. The brooch is nowhere to be found, and Mrs. Cheveley finds out it was Lady Chiltern who forced Robert to write the letter the previous night. Enraged, she tells Lady Chiltern about Robert's past and how he made his fortune selling information. Robert comes in at the end, after Mrs. Cheveley is gone; Lady Chiltern won't forgive him his past. Robert snaps, blaming Lady Chiltern for putting him on an impossible pedestal and ruining his life by forcing him to write that letter.

The third act begins in Lord Goring's house. He receives a letter from Lady Chiltern asking for help. The wording is vague, and the letter could be misinterpreted as from a lover. Just as Lord Goring is expecting Lady Chiltern to call on him, Lord Caversham appears wanting to talk to his son about marriage. Lord Goring sees his father, and, while they are talking, Mrs. Cheveley is admitted by the butler. Since the butler did not know which woman to receive, he mistakenly believed Mrs. Cheveley to be the right one. Mrs. Cheveley, in the drawing room, finds the letter from Lady Chiltern to Lord Goring. She misunderstands and steals the letter.

Meanwhile, Lord Caversham leaves and Sir Robert comes in. Robert is in utter despair and spills his secrets to Lord Goring. Mrs. Cheveley, trying to eavesdrop, knocks over a chair. Robert hears the noise and goes to investigate. Because Mrs. Cheveley and Lord Goring were previously engaged, Robert assumes they are now having an affair and leaves the scene in a huff. Lord Goring, believing Lady Chiltern to be in the drawing room, is surprised to see Mrs. Cheveley.

Mrs. Cheveley wants to offer her hand in marriage to Lord Goring in exchange for Robert's letter. Lord Goring will never accept her because she ruined the Chiltern's love for one another. When Lord Goring finds out she went there looking for a diamond brooch, he pulls it out of a nearby drawer and puts it on her wrist as a bracelet. It turns out Lord Goring gave the brooch to his cousin as a gift, and it was stolen. He threatens to call the police and have Mrs. Cheveley arrested if she does not hand over the letter. She does, and Lord Goring burns it. Before she leaves, however, Mrs. Cheveley reveals that she has stolen the letter from Lady Chiltern and plans to send it to Robert.

The final act shifts back to Robert's house. Lord Caversham is there and tells his son that Robert denounced the canal scheme at the meeting. Lord Goring is waiting for Robert or Lady Chiltern when Mabel enters. They talk, and Lord Goring proposes to her. She accepts and goes outside. Lady Chiltern enters, and Lord Goring tells her the letter is destroyed, but another letter is being sent to Robert. He urges Lady Chiltern to tell Robert the situation, but Lady Chiltern will not. They decide to intercept the letter when Robert comes in holding it.

Since the letter was not addressed to anyone, Robert believed the words to be to him and is overjoyed. Robert and Lady Chiltern reconcile, and Robert agrees to move to the countryside and give up his political life. Lord Caversham comes in, offering Robert a highly-sought position in the cabinet, and Robert goes to write a letter declining the offer. Lord Goring urges Lady Chiltern to allow Robert to stay in politics, as getting him out of London was what Mrs. Chiltern wanted. When Robert comes back, Lady Chiltern tears up the letter.

Robert thanks Lord Goring and asks if there is anything he can do in exchange. Lord Goring asks for Mabel's hand in marriage, and Robert refuses to give it, still believing Lord Goring and Mrs. Cheveley to be having an affair. Lady Chiltern reveals the truth, and Robert gives his permission for the couple to marry.

Themes

Honor

One of the principle discussions of the An Ideal Husband is on the subject of honor and reputation. This is most apparent in the figure of Robert Chiltern, who represents the (seemingly) honest politician. Robert has a virtuous wife, good friends, and an upstanding reputation. Lady Chiltern practically worships Robert for his moral uprightness and considers him nothing without it. Robert's honor is threatened by Mrs. Cheveley dredging up his past. However, he continues to act honorably, not giving in to her threats even if it will cost him his reputation.

The Resurgence of the Past

Several prominent characters throughout the play are forced to confront with aspects of their past, all revolving around Mrs. Cheveley. Lady Chiltern knew Mrs. Cheveley from school, and immediately distrusts her because of her past personality. Lord Goring was once engaged to Mrs. Cheveley, and so she brings back unpleasant memories for him. And Robert is directly confronted with a shameful reminder from his past in the form of the letter in Mrs. Cheveley's possession. The question is whether or not past actions should determine present judgment, and Oscar Wilde seems to lean towards the side of forgiveness for actions.

Ambition and the Definition of Power

The primary conflicts of the play arise because of the character's ambition and quest for power. The philosophy stems from the unseen character Baron Arnheim, whose philosophy of power profoundly affected both Robert Chiltern and Mrs. Cheveley. Both naturally ambitious, Baron Arnheim told them of his philosophy of power, which is centered around wealth. This caused Robert to sell private information and Mrs. Cheveley to try and marry Lord Goring for his fortune. Throughout the play, however, the characters that have the most knowledge, as opposed to the most wealth, hold the true power.

Politics and Corruption

Politics provide the backdrop for the morality struggles of the play. Robert Chiltern is a powerful politician, and his wife educated and involved in his work. They are contrasted by characters such as Lord Goring and Mabel Chiltern, who spurn politics as a general rule. The idea of corruption is considered inherent in politics, and the characters who believe otherwise are viewed as naive. Lord Goring, for instance, tells Lady Chiltern that no political success can be gained without some corruption, and cites it as a reason for her to forgive her husband.

Marriage

Although many other aspects come through in An Ideal Husband, the play itself is still an exploration of the Comedy of Manners and, therefore, centers around the formation of couples. An Ideal Husband goes one step farther than normal Comedy of Manners plays, however, by exploring facets of marriage and relationships. There are two distinct couples who serve as foils to each other: Robert and Lady Chiltern, and Lord Goring and Mabel. The Chilterns, already married, are upright, moral citizens of society concerned with honesty and virtue above all else. Lord Goring and Mabel, on the other hand, are both witty and dismissive of anything serious. In typical fashion, both couples are reconciled at the end of the play.

Women in Society

There are several viewpoints expressed by different characters regarding the role of women in society. The most prominent example of the "ideal wife" is Lady Chiltern. She is virtuous, supportive, educated and politically aware. She is directly contrasted by the "unnatural" Mrs. Cheveley, who is devious and selfish. The older woman, Mrs. Markby, represents the old English society. She believes women should not be educated, as it interferes with marriage. Lady Chiltern disagrees strongly with this, as a modern woman. Women are said throughout the play to be emotion instead of logical, and should play the supportive role in the relationship as opposed to an active role.

Men in Society

Just like women, men are portrayed as having several roles in English society. The ideal role is fulfilled by Robert Chiltern, just as his wife represents the ideal woman. Even though he committed a sin in the past, he remains a powerful yet morally upright man in society. He is ambitious as well as honorable and is a man of intellect. Lord Caversham, of the older generation, approves of Robert Chiltern's way of living. Lord Goring, on the other hand, represents the opposite of Robert. He has no ambitions, is not married, and is overly concerned with appearing young and witty. While his lifestyle is frowned upon by his father, Lord Goring is presented as one of the moral compasses in the play.

Hypocrisy

Many characters in An Ideal Husband portray hypocrisy in their actions and words. Minor characters, such as Lady Basildon, for instance, constantly say one thing to one person, and then a different thing to someone else. Even Lady Chiltern, the most virtuous character in the play, is subject to hypocrisy. Her rules of behavior are so strict that even she cannot follow them, and so, when Lord Goring urges her to tell Robert the truth she refuses for fear of the consequences.

Forgiveness

Only through forgiveness can the conclusion of the play be reached, which was, perhaps, Oscar Wilde's primary purpose in writing the play. Even though characters such as Robert Chiltern committed crimes in their pasts, because they are of value to society, Wilde argues that they should be forgiven based on their merits rather than their sins. In contrast, characters such as Mrs. Cheveley, who have no merits, do not forgive and are not forgiven. There is also the issue of women and forgiveness, since women are seen as putting men on pedestals and not forgiving their faults. This is presented as a "womanly" way to love, and the correct version, the "male" version, requires forgiveness in order to work.

Aestheticism

Oscar Wilde, who helped found the Aestheticism movement and lived a life devoted to the philosophy, puts characters in his plays who believe as he did. In An Ideal Husband, this character, who is a direct representation of Oscar Wilde himself, is Lord Goring. Goring values youth, beauty, and wit and prides himself on his paradoxical views and detachment from politics. Since Lord Goring is not only devoted to a life of pleasure, but also serves as the moral compass for "ideal" characters such as Robert and Lady Chiltern, aestheticism is portrayed in a positive light in the play.

Characters

Sir Robert Chiltern

An accomplished politician with a reputation for being honest and morally upright. Unknown to his wife and society, however, he began his career by selling cabinet secrets to Baron Arnheim. He amassed a sizeable fortune and became successful, when Mrs. Cheveley blackmails him with the letter. Even in the face of losing everything, however, in the end he refuses to give in to her demands. He loves his wife more than anything, and would be willing to sacrifice anything in order to keep her. Robert stands for the "ideal" husband in the play.

Lady Chiltern

Sir Robert Chiltern's wife, Lady Chiltern is also a model member of society. A woman of good breeding and manners, she is always proper and put together. She worships her husband because she believes him to be better than other men and above corruption. When her fantasy is shattered, Lady Chiltern refuses at first to forgive Robert, but eventually realizes that she expected too much of him. Lady Chiltern stands for the "ideal" wife in the play.

Mabel Chiltern

Mabel is Robert Chiltern's younger sister, and a perfect representation of an English beauty. Young, witty and sociable, she is the female "dandy" counterpart to Lord Goring, whom she adores. She doesn't profess any interest in obtaining an ideal husband and thinks she would go insane if she did. She turns down multiple offers of marriage until Lord Goring proposes to her, and she gladly accepts.

Lord Goring

The token dandy bachelor of the play, and Sir Robert's best friend. Thirty-four years old, though claiming thirty-one, Lord Goring is always impeccably dressed no matter the occasion. He has no ambition in life and does not seem to do anything for a living, for which his father repeatedly calls him useless. He enjoys a stylish lifestyle and is constantly calling on other members of high society. Despite his dandy nature, he also acts as a moral compass for characters such as the Chiltern's as they encounter moral entanglements. He represents Aestheticism and, therefore, rebellions against the strict rules of society.

Lord Caversham

Lord Goring's father, Lord Caversham is an elderly gentleman extremely concerned with the traditional rules and standards of society. As such, he and his son do not see eye to eye on any issue, and Lord Caversham constantly dismisses the younger generation as being too modern. While Lord Goring's concerns are style and wit, Lord Caversham is mainly concerned with practicality and common sense.

Mrs. Cheveley

An old schoolmate of Lady Chiltern's who comes back to haunt the cast of the play as the primary villainous character. Mrs. Cheveley is a dangerous combination of beautiful and smart, and travels from Vienna to bribe Robert Chiltern into supporting her fraudulent canal scheme. Lady Chiltern immediately distrusts her because, in school, she was a thief and a liar, and time hasn't changed her terribly much. She manipulates others for her own selfish gain until Lord Goring turns the tables on her by blackmailing her.

Baron Arnheim

Although the Baron never appears on stage (he is dead before the play begins), he still influences the more ambitious characters such as Mrs. Cheveley and Robert Chiltern. He is the one who introduced Robert to his philosophy of power and urged Robert to sell information to him in order to cheat the stock market. The Baron believed that wealth equaled power, and Mrs. Cheveley was his lover and disciple.

Lady Markby

An older friend of the Chiltern family, it is Lady Markby who invites Mrs. Cheveley to the party. Like Lord Caversham, Lady Markby represents the old generation and way of thinking as opposed to the main characters who are all fairly modern. At Lady Chiltern's house, Lady Markby claims not to support the higher education of women because she believes it interferes with a woman's duties and disrupts marriages.

The Countess of Basildon/Mrs. Marchmont

Two frivolous members of society who join the Chiltern's at their party. They talk about pointless things and in general provide comic relief. They represent the shallowness of English society.

Vicomte De Nanjac

A young, awkward man of high society who attends the Chiltern's parties. His awkwardness is contrasted with Lord Goring's wittiness.

Mr. Montford

Robert's secretary, and also a dandy. Lord Goring and Lady Chiltern plan to ask him for the letter, but it was already in Robert's possession.

Mason

The Chiltern's butler. Mason announces the entrance of the characters in the play.

Phipps

Lord Goring's personal butler. Phipps seems absent of all emotion and wears his face like a mask.

James

Lord Goring's footman, escorts Mrs. Cheveley inside.

Harold

Robert Chiltern's footman.

Act Summary

First Act

Setting: The Octagon Room at Sir Robert Chiltern's house in the Grosvenor Square, London

The Chiltern's are hosting a party at their house in London. The entryway is at the top of a grand staircase. Lady Chiltern is at the top of the staircase, greeting the guests. She is elegant and statuesque. At two nearby couches, Mrs. Marchmont and Lady Basildon, two beautiful guests, converse with each other.

Mrs. Marchmont wants to know why they come to these sorts of parties, and Lady Basildon replies that it is to be educated. However, they feel that intelligent conversation is lacking. At dinner, the man Lady Basildon was talking to spent the whole time talking about his wife, and the man Mrs. Marchmont talked to only talked about her qualities. Bored, they leave to go to the music room.

At the top of the staircase, Mason, the Chiltern's Butler, announces Mr. and Mrs. Jane Barford and Lord Caversham. Lord Caversham asks Lady Chiltern after her greeting if she has seen his good-for-nothing son, Lord Goring. Lady Chiltern replies that she hasn't, and Mabel Chiltern, Sir Robert Chiltern's sister, inquires as to why he referred to his own son as "good-for-nothing". Lord Caversham replies that he is idle, yet Mabel points out that he uses all his time socializing. This receives a laugh, and Lord Caversham comments on Mabel's charming nature. He himself is not fond of London society, but Mabel says she enjoys it immensely. Mabel thinks society is formed of "beautiful idiots" and "brilliant lunatics", which is the way it should be. When Lord Caversham asks which category his son falls into, Mabel replies that he has his own category, but she hasn't figured out what it is yet.

Mason announces two more guests, Lady Markby and Mrs. Cheveley, and the scene shifts to the two new women. Lady Chiltern greets Lady Markby warmly, and Lady Markby tries to introduce her to Mrs. Cheveley. Lady Chiltern at first is friendly and then, upon a closer look, bows coldly to Mrs. Cheveley, saying they've met before. Mrs. Cheveley feigns innocence, saying she cannot place her. Lady Chiltern reminds her that they went to school together and asks why she has come to London. When Mrs. Cheveley replies she says that it was to meet Lady Chiltern's husband, Sir Robert Chiltern. At this, Lady Chiltern replies that Mrs. Cheveley cannot have any relevant business with her husband, and departs.

The Vicomte De Nanjac, a young French gentleman, approaches Mrs. Cheveley and tells her that it is been a long time. The last time they saw each other was in Berlin, five years ago. He tells her she is beautiful, and she accuses him of flattery.

Sir Robert Chiltern enters. He has a distinct air, and a strong personality which demands respect. He wants to know who Mrs. Cheveley is, and Mabel introduces them. Mrs. Cheveley came to London from Vienna, and she and Sir Robert enter into conversation. He compliments her and offers to introduce her to his wife, but Mrs. Cheveley replies that the two knew each other in school. She believes Lady Chiltern got rewards for good behavior, but Mrs. Cheveley didn't receive good marks. Sir Robert, being polite, tells her that she should have gotten a reward for being charming, and Mrs. Cheveley, once again saying the unexpected, remarks that being charming only punishes women instead of helping them. Sir Robert, keeping up with the witty reply, asks if she is an optimist or a pessimist. She says that she is neither and that science can't possibly understand women as they are too irrational.

She tells Sir Robert that she came to London for the sole purpose of meeting him, and to ask him a favor. She is in politics, and tells him that she will ask the question later. She instead changes the conversation, asking for a tour of his beautiful home and dropping the name Baron Arnheim into the conversation. At the mention of this name, Sir Robert starts and asks if she knew the later Baron. She says yes she knew him well and wants to know if Sir Robert knew him. Sir Robert did, and agreed that he was a remarkable man.

Lord Goring enters the room. He is a young dandy who does not like to be taken seriously and enjoys witty conversation. Sir Robert Chiltern introduces Lord Goring to Mrs. Cheveley as "the idlest man in London". Mrs. Cheveley says she doesn't need an introduction because they have met before. Lord Goring is surprised that she remembered him, and she tells him that her memory is flawless. She then, somewhat mockingly, asks Lord Goring if he is still a bachelor. He is, and she sarcastically pins it as romantic.

Mrs. Cheveley leaves with Sir Robert and Lord
Goring walks over to Mabel Chiltern. Mabel playfully
accuses him of being late, and they engage in witty,
lighthearted conversation about Lord Goring many
bad qualities and how Mabel would not get rid of any
of them. Lord Goring asks Mabel who invited Mrs.
Cheveley, and Mabel tells him it was Lady Markby.
Mabel then remarks that she doesn't like Mrs.
Cheveley, and Lord Goring tells her she has good
taste.

Vicomte joins the conversation here,
misunderstanding the "good taste" comment. Lord
Goring insults him, saying he needs to read between
the lines. The Vicomte asks Mabel to accompany him
to the music room, and Mabel is disappointed. She
agrees anyway, however, and asks Lord Goring if he
is coming, as well. When he answers no, Mabel walks
away resigned.

Lord Caversham comes up to his son, complaining
that parties such as this are a waste of time and that
everyone talks about nothing. Goring claims to like
talking about nothing, and Lord Caversham gets on to
him about his wasteful life as a dandy, going to
parties and living only for pleasure. Lord Goring tells
his father that he cannot imagine another way to live.

Lady Basildon comes up, and Mrs. Marchmont following and is surprised to see Lord Goring at a political party. The conversation turns from politics to husbands, and Lady Basildon and Mrs. Marchmont both complain that they have married perfect husbands and are miserable for it. While their husbands are happy and trusting, their wives complain that they are bored. Lord Goring brings up Mrs. Cheveley, saying that she is a handsome woman. Lady Basildon and Mrs. Marchmont both get onto him, as they don't like her.

Mabel comes back from the music room and joins the conversation. She complains that everyone is doing nothing but talking about Mrs. Cheveley and asks Lord Goring to escort her to dinner. When they walk away, Mabel gets on to Goring for not following her to the music room.

Mrs. Marchmont and Lady Basildon decide that they want dinner, as well. The Vicomte De Nanjac asks to take Lady Basildon to supper. She replies that she won't eat, but she will be happy to accompany him. Mr. Montford, another dandy, offers to take Mrs. Marchmont. Mrs. Marchmont refuses to eat but says she will watch him eat.

When everyone else is gone to supper, Sir Robert Chiltern and Mrs. Cheveley sit down to talk on the couches. Sir Robert wants to know how long Mrs. Cheveley is planning on staying in England, and Mrs. Cheveley tells him that it depends on his actions. Confused, Mrs. Cheveley begins explaining.

She is involved in the Argentine Canal Project and has invested heavily in it on advice from Baron Arnheim, the man mentioned before. Sir Robert tells her that the Argentine Canal Project is a scam and he is going tomorrow to submit papers to the council revealing it as such. Mrs. Cheveley offers to pay Sir Robert if he inserts positive information into the report, to allow the canal to be built. He is indignant about this and asks her to leave.

Before she goes, she tells Sir Robert that she knows he got his wealth and successful career by selling Cabinet secrets to the Stock Exchange. She has a letter from Baron Arnheim proving it. Sir Robert claims the letter is just speculation, but he is nervous. He tells her that he will not do what she asks, to give false information to the council, but she threatens to expose him and create a scandal. She admits that she is currently his enemy, but also acknowledges that she has the upper hand in the situation because she is attacking, and he defending. She tells him that people always pay for their wrongs, so he has to do what she asks.

Once again, Sir Robert tells her that it is impossible. In response, Mrs. Cheveley makes a move to leave, imagining out loud how eager the local news junkies would be to receive such a big scoop. Robert tells her to wait and asks for the terms, to stop the report and give a short speech on the economic possibilities of the canal. Mrs. Cheveley says those are the correct terms and waits for him to respond. He offers to pay her any sum of money instead of lying to the council, but she refuses.

She tells Robert that she will be waiting at the Ladies Gallery with the letter in hand tomorrow night. If, by that time, he has gone through with her terms, she will give the letter to him so that no trace of his past dishonesty remains in the world. He must decide tonight, and go through with the deed tomorrow if he wants to receive the letter. Robert, beaten, agrees to her arrangement. She asks him to call her carriage, and he leaves to do so.

When Sir Robert is gone, the guests reenter. Lady Markby comments to Mrs. Cheveley about how noble and entertaining Sir Robert is. She invites Mrs. Cheveley to ride in the Park with her tomorrow before leaving. Lady Chiltern comes up to Mrs. Cheveley next, wanting to know what business she had with her husband. Mrs. Cheveley tells her that she came to discuss the Argentine Canal Project, to which Lady Chiltern replies that her husband would never agree to invest in such an obvious fraud. Mrs. Cheveley tells her that she is mistaken and that the deal is already settled. She also states that, until tomorrow night, the terms are a secret between Sir Robert and herself.

Sir Robert comes back in with the announcement that Mrs. Cheveley's carriage is waiting. He escorts her out of the room, and Lady Chiltern watches from the top of the staircase, deeply troubled.

In the other reception room, Mabel is expressing her bad opinion of Mrs. Cheveley. She sits down on the couch to talk to Lord Goring and sees something shiny in the cracks. When she pulls it out, it is a beautiful diamond brooch. Lord Goring, taking close notice, states that it could be a bracelet and asks to see it. When Mabel gives it to him, he puts it in his breast pocket. Mabel looks at him, and he asks to make a strange request. Eagerly, Mabel responds that she has been waiting for just that. Slightly taken aback, he asks her to keep his possession of the brooch a secret and to let him know if anyone inquires about it. When she asks why, he tells her that he gave the brooch to someone a long time ago.

Lady Chiltern comes back alone, as the other guests have all gone home. Mabel excuses herself, and Lord Goring is left. He and Lady Chiltern, who both knew Mrs. Cheveley in the past and don't seem to like her, wonder why she came to London. They express misfortune at her appearance, and wonder what she is up to with regards to Sir Robert Chiltern. Lady Chiltern is sure that her husband would never have invested in the canal project, and thinks Mrs. Cheveley is stupid.

Lord Goring leaves, and Robert returns from escorting Mrs. Cheveley out. Lady Chiltern asks him if it is true that he is aiding the canal project, and Sir Robert, startled, asks her who told her. Lady Chiltern replies that Mrs. Cheveley told her, and goes on to say that she knows from her years spend with Mrs. Cheveley in school that she is evil and a thief. Sir Robert hints that maybe she has changed, and his Lady tells him that a person's past is their person. She senses that he is not telling her the whole truth about the incident, and wants to know why Robert is keeping things from her.

Sitting down, he explains that politics and truth are complicated matters, and can vary based on multiple circumstances. He tells his Lady that he had to compromise with Mrs. Cheveley on his stance regarding the canal. Lady Chiltern is upset and states that he is a man known for his honor, unsullied by the ways of the world, and that it is never necessary to compromise one's principles. She realizes that there are some men who have horrible secrets in her past and must do terrible things to keep them in the dark. She hopes her husband isn't one of these men and asks him for the truth so she can know whether or not to stay with him.

Sir Robert tells her that she knows everything there is to know about his past and agrees, with prompting, to write a letter to Mrs. Cheveley that night stating his intention to be honest and submit the report. After Lady Chiltern is satisfied with the letter, she gives it to Mason with order to take it to Mrs. Cheveley's hotel. Mason leaves, and Lady Chiltern is grateful to her husband for doing the right thing. She leaves, and a servant begins putting out the lights.

Second Act

The morning room at Sir Robert Chiltern's house.

Lord Goring is pacing the room, distressed. When Robert walks in Lord Goring tells him that he shouldn't have kept his secret of his success from her. Robert reveals to Lord Goring that if he would have told the Lady Chiltern his secret last night she would have left him for good. Goring, not having realized Robert's predicament, apologizes and offers to talk to Lady Chiltern for him to smooth things over. Robert is convinced that talking to her would not do any good, and would be too risky.

Robert is ashamed at what he did in his past, yet excuses himself somewhat by saying that others have done far worse in their pursuit of wealth and that he didn't hurt anybody. Lord Goring is quiet for a moment, and tells him that he has hurt himself. The inevitable conclusion to such an act was always a scandal. It does not matter that Robert was only twenty-two at the time of its occurrence or that his morals are otherwise perfectly sound.

Lord Goring asks Robert how he came to give up such valuable information in the first place, and Robert tells him. One night, fresh out of school, well-bred but poor, he had a late-night conversation with Baron Arnheim. The Baron, an extremely wealthy man, revealed to Robert his philosophy on life, which is, wealth is power. According to the Baron, the luxury wealth allows one to experience is nothing in comparison to the power wielded over men and offices. He then asked Robert to let him know if he came across any valuable information at his job. Robert, highly ambitious at the time, came across some state papers six weeks later and sold them to the Baron for a small fortune.

Lord Goring interrupts Robert to say that the Baron Arnheim's philosophy seems shallow and that Robert's action showed a weakness on his part. Robert defends himself by replying that, to some extent, the Baron's philosophy on life is true, as Robert's now-immense wealth has afforded him enormous power. He also says that taking the sort of risk that he did had courage in it, since he could have lost everything he had worked for in one move.

Robert continues his story. In five years time, he had tripled his worth. He tells Lord Goring that he does not regret his action, as the action of gaining wealth is equivalent to a war, and he simply used a weapon that was given to him to get started. Since then, he has donated many times that to public charities.

Lord Goring is thoughtful after hearing Robert's story. He mulls over what to do, ruling out confession, as it would ruin Robert's good reputation, and deciding that the only way out is to fight. That fight would start, Goring insists, by telling Lady Chiltern. Robert, however, shoots that down and instead sends a letter of inquiry to Mrs. Cheveley's home country in order to find some scandalous bit of information about her to counter her attack. He rings the bell and gives Mason the letter, and they hear his wife's footsteps in the hall.

Lady Chiltern walks in and greets the two men. She says that she wants to talk to Lord Goring about some business after she goes to take off her bonnet. Lord Goring, being witty, says he would rather talk about her bonnet. She leaves the room, promising to come back in a few minutes.

Robert and Lord Goring continue their conversation. Robert tells Goring that he has been a good friend. Confused, Goring replies that he has not done Robert anything of worth thus far. To this, Robert says he has allowed him to get the truth off his chest, and that is a powerful relief. Lord Goring tells Robert that he is going to the Bachelor's Ball tonight if Robert needs to get ahold of him for any reason.

Robert gets up to leave, and just as he does his wife walks in the room. She asks him if he must go. He tells her that he has some letters to write, and she replies that he works too much. After Robert is out of the room, Lady Chiltern sits down, and Lord Goring sits down with her. Lord Goring assumes that she wants to talk about not bonnets or business but Mrs. Cheveley. He assumes right, and the Lady Chiltern goes over the situation again to Lord Goring, including the part about her making Robert write the letter.

Lord Goring is quiet through her explanation, and Lady Chiltern, picking up on this, asks him if Robert has anything to hide. Goring tries to talk delicately, saying that in practical life some things happen. Lady Chiltern upholds her stance of her husband as never committing wrong, and Goring tells her that in ambition and success there must be certain allowances for behavior. He is trying to soften Lady Chiltern up to tell her the truth, or at least hint at it, and when she protests he tells her that her morals are too severe.

Lord Goring presents a hypothetical situation of a young man writing a foolish letter that might compromise his position. Lady Chiltern protests that her husband would not do something foolish, and Goring tells her that everyone is capable of committing foolish acts. She calls him a pessimist, and he, passionate, tells her that he is not pessimistic and that he believes love to be the explanation for life. At the end of his speech, he offers to help her if she ever needs it. Lady Chiltern is surprised because she has never heard him talk seriously before.

Mabel Chiltern enters in a beautiful, elaborate dress. She inserts into the conversation, saying that seriousness doesn't suit Lord Goring at all. Goring greets her and then apologizes, saying he must leave. Mabel accuses him of having poor manners and reminds him that they are supposed to go riding tomorrow at eleven. Lord Goring, turning to Lady Chiltern, asks for her guest list, saying it was not in the papers. Lady Chiltern tells him that Tommy Trafford, Robert's secretary, can provide it. Thanking her, Lord Goring reminds her to remember their conversation before leaving.

Mabel, disappointed that Lord Goring is gone, begins talking to Lady Chiltern. She complains that Robert needs to get rid of Tommy Trafford because he won't stop proposing to her. While she is fond of him, she says his methods of proposing are totally unromantic. Lady Chiltern, trying to cheer her up, states that Tommy is a brilliant man with a bright future and says that she might take his proposals seriously. Mabel replies that she can't stand men with futures or geniuses and that she is going to visit Lady Basildon at her house. She leaves the room and comes back hurriedly, asking if Lady Chiltern had invited Mrs. Cheveley. Lady Chiltern is surprised as Mabel reveals that she and Mrs. Markby are coming up the stairs.

Just then, Mason walks in the room announcing both Mrs. Markby and Mrs. Cheveley. Lady Chiltern greets Mrs. Markby affectionately, and once again bows coldly to Mrs. Cheveley. Mrs. Cheveley says she has not yet met Mabel, though she saw her last night. She also throws out a thinly veiled insult, stating that the dress Mabel wore previously was simpler and more fitting. Mabel ignores the slight and announces that she is leaving. When the two guests press her to stay, she reveals that it is an obligation to charity. She is working with Lord Goring and Tommy Trafford. Mrs. Markby tells her that, while charity work is essential, being pretty is the most crucial thing for a modern woman. Mabel politely excuses herself.

When Mabel is gone, Lady Markby asks Lady Chiltern if a diamond brooch was found after the party last night. The brooch belongs to Mrs. Cheveley, and she is searching desperately for it. Lady Chiltern does not know if a brooch was found, and summons Mason to double-check. She gives a description of the brooch, a diamond snake with a large ruby. He does not know of a brooch that was found either, and Mrs. Cheveley says she must have lost it at the Opera before dinner. Lady Chiltern sends Mason out to fetch tea.

While Mason it out, Mrs. Markby begins making small talk. She expresses several opinions with obviously irk Lady Chiltern. One of them is about she doesn't support the Higher Education of Women, and Lady Chiltern tells her that both she and her husband are involved in the project. She also complains about her husband, and about how he is so involved in politics. Mrs. Markby hates to listen to him rant, and Lady Chiltern tells her that she herself is involved in the political sphere and enjoys discussing things with her husband. Markby, going on, oblivious, complains that her husband, John, is obsessed with reading the Blue Books. Mrs. Cheveley remarks slyly that she would rather read books with yellow colors.

Mason comes back in with the tea and serves Mrs. Cheveley. Mrs. Markby refuses any tea, since she must make another visit to Lady Brancaster, whose husband has died recently. She invites Mrs. Cheveley to come with her and wait in the carriage, but Lady Chiltern insists that Mrs. Cheveley stays as they have something to discuss. She doesn't plan on seeing Mrs. Markby that night, as she and Robert are dining at home.

She tells Mason to see Mrs. Markby out, and turns on Mrs. Cheveley. She tells Mrs. Cheveley that if she had known who she was last night she never would have invited her to the party. She goes on to accuse Mrs. Cheveley of being dishonorable and gives a speech about how, when a person is dishonorable once, it is certain that they will be again. Mrs. Cheveley asks if Lady Chiltern would apply that policy to everyone, and Lady Chiltern says yes.

Mrs. Cheveley says that she is sorry and that she wishes to talk morality with Lady Chiltern. During the argument, Lady Chiltern reveals that she was the one who made Robert write the letter calling off the arrangement. Mrs. Cheveley grows angry and tells her that she must make him change his mind on the matter. Lady Chiltern asks her how she knows her husband well enough to make outrageous demands, and Mrs. Cheveley replies that she knows him because they are alike. They are both dishonest people. When Lady Chiltern, fed up with the argument, orders Mrs. Cheveley to leave, Mrs. Cheveley tells her that her husband made his fortune by selling state intelligence.

Robert, entering, hears the last of Mrs. Cheveley's accusations and turns pale. Mrs. Cheveley, seeing him, asks him to deny it. When he doesn't deny the allegations, Lady Chiltern becomes upset. She rings the bell to summon Mason and asks him to show Mrs. Cheveley out, and to never let her come in again. She leaves.

After she is gone, Lady Chiltern turns to Robert. She wants to know if it is true. He says that it is and begins his explanation, but she cuts him off, saying he is worse than a common thief. Robert rushes towards her, trying to comfort her, but she pushes him back. He then gets angry. He tells her that it is her fault he had to keep things from her because she expected him to be perfect. She worshipped him and put him on a pedestal that no person could live up to. He goes on to say that men accept women's imperfections and love them and that women should do the same for men. He accuses her of making a false idol out of him and by ruining his life when he had a chance to redeem his shameful past forever. Now, the only thing left for him is to lose everything he has worked for and live life with a dishonorable reputation. Robert leaves the room, and Lady Chiltern rushes to the door after him. When she reaches it, however, it has already closed. She lies down on the sofa and begins to sob.

Third Act

The library in Lord Goring's house.

Phipps, the butler, is arranging the room. Lord Goring enters, well-dressed, and asks Phipps to help him with his button-hole. Lord Goring philosophizes about life while Phipps agrees with him in a formal, polite manner. Goring notices that there are some new letters on the table, and recognizes Lady Chiltern's handwriting on one of them. He opens it and reads "I trust you. I want you. I am coming to see you". Lord Goring immediately realizes that Lady Chiltern has somehow found out about her husband's scandal. Although he had plans for dinner, he decides not to go, and to wait up for Lady Chiltern instead.

Just then, Phipps enters, announcing Lord Caversham. Lord Goring's father enters, taking off his cloak and settling in a comfortable chair. He tells Goring that he has come to have a serious conversation. Lord Goring replies that tonight is not a good night, as he can only be serious on Tuesdays. Lord Caversham is frustrated and continues with his main point. He wants his son to be married, as he is thirty-four and still a bachelor. He says that being a bachelor is unfashionable now and tells Goring to look at Robert Chiltern and take him as a role-model. He married a well-bred woman and has never been better off.

Goring tells him that he will take Robert as a model, and that he is more than willing to have a conversation about marriage, but for now Lord Caversham must leave. The old gentleman refuses and complains of a draft in the library. Lord Goring tells him that they can move to the smoking-room, where there is a fire going. Lord Caversham goes out, grumbling.

Lord Goring goes to Phipps, telling him that he is expecting a lady to come over. When she arrives, he is to put her in the drawing room and let no one else in the house. He tells Phipps that it is a matter of utmost importance. The bell rings, and Goring says he will get it himself. Before he reaches the door, however, Lord Caversham comes back out of the smoking room, wondering what is taking him so long. Lord Goring goes with his father.

Harold, the footman, brings Mrs. Cheveley in. When she asks about Lord Goring, Phipps tells her that he is presently engaged in a conversation with his father but that she can wait in the drawing room until he is done. Mrs. Caversham is surprised that Lord Goring was "expecting" her, and immediately concluded that he must be having an affair with another woman.

Looking in the drawing room, she complains that there is not enough light, and sends Phipps to get some more candles. When the butler is gone, she notices the letter on Lord Goring's desk. She recognizes Lady Chiltern's handwriting and reads the note. Her face becomes triumphant, and she moves to put the letter in her bag. Before she can, Phipps comes back in with the candles, and she hides the letter.

When Mrs. Cheveley is in the drawing room, Phipps retires. The drawing room door opens slowly, and Mrs. Cheveley emerges, creeping toward the table where the letter is. She hears voices and stops. The voices get louder, and she goes back into the drawing room.

Lord Goring and Lord Caversham enter, continuing their conversation about marriage. Lord Goring wants to know if he will at least be able to pick his future bride, and Lord Caversham says no. He thinks his son will pick someone who he loves, which will be a disaster. He believes a happy marriage will end with affection, which is what Lord Goring believes couples say they have when they no longer like each other. Lord Caversham plans on using common sense, rather than love, to pick at mate for Lord Goring. Goring shows his father out the door.

When he comes back in, Sir Robert Chiltern is with him. Robert says he is lucky he saw him on the doorstep because Phipps told him the Goring wasn't home. Lord Goring tries to excuse himself by saying that he is busy, but Robert won't leave. He tells Goring that his wife has discovered his secret and that his life is ruined. When Lord Goring asks what happened, Robert tells him that Mrs. Cheveley herself told Lady Chiltern. After telling the story, he buries his face in his hands.

Lord Goring tries to think of things to do and asks if he has received any reply from his letter about Mrs. Cheveley yet. A letter came back, but Mrs. Cheveley is a member of high society with no scandals about her. The Baron Arnheim left her most of his sizeable fortune. Losing hope, Goring offers Robert a drink. When Phipps comes in with the order, Lord Goring tells him when the lady comes to call to send her away. Phipps reveals that "she" is already in the room. Knowing the situation has become a mess, Lord Goring decides to try and get Robert to leave.

Going back to Robert, Goring listens to him talk. He is in despair because he loves his wife and doesn't have anybody else. They did not have any children. Lord Goring asks him if he loves his wife, and Robert says he does. He used to believe ambition the greatest thing to have in life, but now he believes it is love. He tells Goring he was brutal to his Lady earlier today, and Goring says she must forgive him despite his wrongs.

Lord Goring, delicately changing the subject, asks Robert if his carriage is here, and says he needs him to leave for a while. Robert says he needs to stay because he still doesn't know what to do and the debate about the Argentine Canal is at eleven o'clock. As he says this, he hears something fall in the drawing room. Lord Goring tries to tell him that it was nothing, but Robert believes someone has been eavesdropping. He sees the door is ajar and the light open, but Goring swears on his honor that no one is there. When Robert insists on opening the door to the room, Lord Goring forbids it. Robert wants to know what he has to hide, and Goring admits there is someone in the room who Robert must not see. Robert goes in the room anyway and comes back out angry.

Lord Goring, thinking Robert has seen his wife, tries to explain. He tells Robert that she is guiltless of any crime and is here because she loves him. Robert calls him mad and tells Goring she will make a choice mistress for him because they are so well-suited for each other. Before Lord Goring can say anything else, Robert leaves.

When he opens the drawing room door, Mrs. Cheveley walks out looking amused. Lord Goring asks her what she was doing, and she tells him she was listening through the door. He takes off her cloak and offers her a cigarette, which she refuses. He guesses that she is here to sell him Robert's letter of condemnation and wants to know the price. Mrs. Cheveley tells Goring that she has plenty of money and that she wants something else.

She tells him she wants to move back to London and live a more simple life. If Lord Goring agrees to marry her, she will give him the letter tomorrow. Lord Goring replies that he would make a bad husband, and she replies that she loves bad husbands. Seeing that he is not inclined to accept her offer, she tells him that if he does not she will reveal Robert's scandal and ruin his life. She knows his true character and says he will be getting the punishment he deserves.

Lord Goring defends his friend, telling her that Robert's act was done when he was young and foolish, and not his true character. He gets on to her, saying that, while she claimed to come to him for love, earlier that day she desecrated love by deliberately telling Lady Chiltern about Robert, turning the happy couple against each other. This is something Lord Goring says he cannot forgive.

Mrs. Cheveley defends herself, saying that it is not her fault. She went to the Chiltern house to look for her brooch, which she lost. Lord Goring asks her if it is a diamond snake with a ruby, and, surprised, Mrs. Cheveley answers yes. Lord Goring goes over to a drawer and pulls the brooch out, saying that he found it but forgot to tell the butler. Mrs. Cheveley expresses her thanks, saying the brooch is crucial to her because it was a gift. She asks Lord Goring to pin it on her, and Lord Goring instead uses it as a bracelet. Mrs. Cheveley is surprised again and asks how he knew it could be worn in such a fashion. Lord Goring reveals that the brooch was a present from him to Lady Berkshire, ten years ago on her wedding day.

Mrs. Cheveley goes pale. Lord Goring goes on to accuse her of stealing it, and Mrs. Cheveley tries to take it off. When she cannot find the clasp she panics and begins calling Lord Goring names. He says he is going to call his servant, and that the police will be there shortly to arrest Mrs. Cheveley of thievery. The next day he is sure the Berkshires will try her, unless Mrs. Cheveley gives him the letter condemning Robert Chiltern. After some excuses, she hands the letter over, and Lord Goring burns it in the fire.

While the original letter is burning, Mrs. Cheveley sees the corner of the second letter, the one from Lady Chiltern, sticking out from its hiding place. Asking Lord Goring for a glass of water, she grabs the letter while his back is turned. When he tries to give her the water, she asks instead for her cloak and carriage. She tells Goring that she no longer intends to harm Robert, but instead do him a service and show him Lady Chiltern's love letter. Confused, Lord Goring asks what she means, and Mrs. Cheveley pulls out the letter written earlier that day. Goring swears to get the letter back, by force if he has to, but before he can do anything Mrs. Cheveley rings the bells. Phipps comes in, and Mrs. Cheveley asks him to escort her out. Looking back at Lord Goring, her expression is triumphant.

Fourth Act

Morning room at Sir Robert Chiltern's house.

Lord Goring is standing before the fireplace, checking his watch and looking bored. He rings the bells and the servant comes in. Lord Goring asks if anyone is available, but the servant says that Robert is still at the office, and Miss Chiltern has just gotten back from riding, but is still in her room. However, Lord Caversham is in the library waiting for Robert. Lord Goring tells the servant not to tell his father he is here, since he doesn't want to see the man three days in a row.

He sits down to read the paper when Lord Caversham walks in. He wants to know if his son has thought about their conversation at all, and Lord Goring replies that he has. He hopes to be engaged before lunchtime. Lord Caversham asks Lord Goring if he has read The Times this morning, and Lord Goring has not. There is an article in the paper about Robert Chiltern's political career. Lord Goring worries until his father goes on to say that it was a positive article regarding how he denounced the Argentine Canal project as a scam at that night's meeting. Lord Goring is delighted at the news, and Lord Caversham turns the subject back to marriage. He asks if Goring is planning on proposing to Miss Chiltern, and Lord Goring answers that Mabel would be too good for him.

Just as they are speaking about her, Mabel enters the room. She greets Lord Caversham, inquiring about the health of his wife. Lord Goring greets her, but she ignores him and continues talking to his father. Clearing his throat, Lord Goring tries again. This time Mabel looks up in mock surprise and asks what he wants. Since he didn't keep his riding appointment with her she doesn't plan on speaking to him again. She asks Lord Caversham if he can teach his son any manners, but Lord Caversham says it is useless. He glares at Lord Goring and goes out.

Mabel begins arranging the flowers in the room, and complains about Lord Goring missing the ride. He says he is sorry, but he looks pleased. When Mabel asks why, he tells her he has something important to say. She asks if it is a proposal and Goring, startled, says yes. Mabel then exclaims that this will be her second proposal today, and Goring is mad that someone proposed before him. She says that Tommy Trafford proposed again, but she didn't accept him. Lord Goring is glad, and expresses his love for Mabel. He wants to know if she loves him in return, and she, laughing, says she has adored him for months.

They kiss and enjoy a blissful moment together. Lord Goring tells Mabel that he is not good enough for her, and that he is over thirty as well as ridiculously extravagant. Mabel tells him that she never wanted someone who was good enough for her, that he looks a few weeks shy of thirty, and that she is extravagant as well.

Lady Chiltern comes in, and Mabel tells Lord Goring that she is going to the conservatory and will wait for him under the second palm tree. She blows a kiss to him on the way out of the room. Lord Goring sits on the sofa with Lady Chiltern, and tells her that there is good news. The letter against Robert has been burned, but Mrs. Caversham stole the letter which Lady Chiltern wrote him and plans to use it against her. Lady Chiltern is first happy, then alarmed. She cannot believe that someone would infer an affair from the contents of the letter, and asks Goring to tell the whole story.

When Goring is done, he advises Lady Chiltern to go to Robert and tell him everything at once. Lady Chiltern immediately looks terrified and says that is impossible, as it would be improper for Lord Goring to have been expecting Lady Chiltern at such a later hour. Lord Goring tells her it would be wrong not to tell him, but Lady Chiltern continues freaking out. Lord Goring tells her to calm down, and asks what other options they have. Lady Chiltern thinks the only solution is to intercept the letter before it gets to Robert. Robert's secretary that day is Mr. Montford, and Lord Goring wants to make sure Lady Chiltern trusts him before they go to intercept the letter. She says she does, and Lord Goring is planning on visiting Mr. Montford immediately.

Before he can leave, however, they hear Robert Chiltern coming up the stairs. He has the letter in his hands and rushes to Lady Chiltern, not even noticing Lord Goring. Robert asks her if the letter is true, if she really wants and trusts him. Robert has misunderstood the letter, thinking it was meant for him instead of someone else. Lord Goring makes a sign to Lady Chiltern, telling her to go along with his misunderstanding.

Lord Goring, still unnoticed by Robert, slips out of the room and heads towards the conservatory. Robert and Lady Chiltern continue their conversation and Lady Chiltern tells Robert the latest news, that the offending letter from his past has been destroyed. Robert is shocked and pleased, and wants to know how it happened. Lady Chiltern tells him that it was Lord Goring who conned Mrs. Cheveley out of the letter and, once it was safely in his possession, burned it. Robert is glad, but also wishes that he could have seen it burning with his own eyes because it would have been satisfying.

Robert then asks his wife what they should do now that the whole debacle is over with. He suggests retiring public life and moving out to the country. Lady Chiltern agrees, and tells him that would make her immensely happy. He seems a little hurt, since Lady Chiltern was once his strongest ally for his political ambition, and supported what he was trying to do in office. Lady Chiltern tells him that they should disregard ambition, as it only brought them trouble. The letter was a prime example of that, and she suggests they learn from their mistakes and lead a more simple life. Robert seems sad, but pleased that Lady Chiltern is happy.

As they wrap up their conversation, Lord Goring comes back in from the conservatory looking pleased with himself. Robert goes to him, shaking his hand and thanking him. He tells Lord Goring that he doesn't know how to repay him for destroying the letter.

Lord Goring is about to speak when Mason enters, announcing Lord Caversham. Lord Caversham congratulates Robert before telling him that his speech on the Argentine Canal has earned him a seat on the Cabinet. Robert is astonished, and Lord Caversham gives him the letter of recommendation from the Prime Minister. Joyous, Robert is about to accept the position when he glances at his wife and sees her pleading look. He then hands the letter back and tells Lord Caversham that he plans to decline the position and leave society for the country.

Lord Caversham is flabbergasted, and pleads with Lady Chiltern to change his mind, as she is a "sensible" woman. When Lady Chiltern not only supports Robert's decision but expresses admiration for it, Lord Caversham declares them all mad. Lady Chiltern ignores Lord Caversham and turns to Robert, telling him that he must write his response to the Prime Minister immediately. Robert tells her he will go write it, but says it with a touch of bitterness. Lady Chiltern accompanies him out.

Lord Caversham tells his son that the Chiltern's are being idiotic, but Lord Goring tells him that they are exhibiting a high moral character. He tells his father that there is someone who he needs to see in the conservatory, and to go there. Lord Caversham leaves the room, and Lady Chiltern enters.

Lord Goring asks Lady Chiltern why she is playing right into Mrs. Cheveley's hand. By asking Robert to give up his public life and retire to the country, isn't Lady Chiltern accomplishing what Mrs. Cheveley started? Lord Goring continues on to say that Lady Chiltern asks for his help and advice, and that she must listen to him now. He tells her not to take away all that Robert has worked his whole life for because, even if they move out of the public sphere for love, that sacrifice will eventually poison their relationship. He acknowledges that Robert would do anything to keep Lady Chiltern by his side, including sacrificing a once-in-a-lifetime opportunity, but she should not let him.

Robert enters the room with the first draft of his letter for Lady Chiltern to go over. He hands the paper to her, and she reads it. Then, she tears it up. Robert is surprised, but Lady Chiltern says that after talking with Lord Goring she realized she didn't want Robert to sacrifice everything he'd worked for. Once again, Robert expresses thanks to his best friend for clearing up his seemingly impossible problems.

Lord Goring tells Robert that if he genuinely wants to repay him, then he will consent to Lord Goring marrying his sister, Mabel. Lady Chiltern is overjoyed, and begins congratulating Lord Goring. Robert, however, is angry. He tells Lord Goring that he won't sacrifice Mabel to someone who doesn't love her. Lord Goring assures Robert of his love for Mabel, and wants to know the reason for not giving consent to the marriage. Robert, still under the mistaken conclusion that Lord Goring and Mrs. Cheveley are having an affair, tells Lord Goring that he cannot possibly love both. Lord Goring accepts this reasoning, still keeping Lady Chiltern's secret from Robert.

Lady Chiltern, to save the situation, reveals what actually happened that night. When Robert learns that Lord Goring did not know Mrs. Cheveley was in his drawing room that night, Robert forgives him and happily gives his consent for Lord Goring to marry Mabel.

Mabel enters the room with Lord Caversham. Lord Goring goes to her and kisses her passionately. Lord Caversham is shocked, and immediately understands that Lord Goring has proposed, and Mabel accepted. Robert also tells Lord Caversham that he has changed his mind, and will accept the Cabinet seat. Lord Caversham is glad, and says that they have some sense after all.

Mason enters and announces to the group that lunch is ready to be served. They talk for a few minutes more, and Lord Caversham tells Lord Goring that he needs to make Mabel the ideal husband. Mabel says she doesn't need Lord Goring to be the ideal husband, because that would be boring. But she wants to be an ideal wife for him. Lord Caversham says that they will have an illustrious future together and make each other happy.

Everyone leaves the room except for Robert. He sits alone, lost in thought. Lady Chiltern comes back in to check on him, and asks if anything is the matter. Robert wants to know if Lady Chiltern stayed with him out of love or pity. Lady Chiltern assures him that she stayed out of love.

About BookCaps

We all need refreshers every now and then. Whether you are a student trying to cram for that big final, or someone just trying to understand a book more, BookCaps can help. We are a small, but growing company, and are adding titles every month.

Visit www.bookcaps.com to see more of our books, or contact us with any questions.

Printed in Poland
by Amazon Fulfillment
Poland Sp. z o.o., Wrocław

51607449R00043

LEADING THE WAY

A new vision for local government

by
Rt Hon Tony Blair MP

INSTITUTE FOR PUBLIC POLICY RESEARCH

CONTENTS

Preface

The reform of government and, in particular, the revitalisation of local government are firmly on the UK political agenda, as this booklet makes clear. These are areas in which the IPPR has long taken a particular interest. Among the Institute's earliest publications were John Stewart's tract, *An experiment in freedom: The case for free local authorities in Britain* and James Cornford's sweeping synopsis and proposal for *The Constitution of the United Kingdom*. More recently the IPPR's government programme has been examining current issues in reform and completed *The Greater London Authority: principles and structure*, dealing with innovations in local and regional governmnent and their application to the capital.

We are delighted to publish this contribution to the debate on local government reform from the pen of the Prime Minister. It sets out his view of the issues and priorities for change and shows the avenues along which his thoughts are running. Essentially, he argues for a separation of the executive from the representative role in local government both to clarify accountability for executive decisions and to develop greater powers of leadership in local affairs.

The views expressed are, of course, his and should not be interpreted as the position of the IPPR, its staff or trustees.

Gerald Holtham
Director

Executive Summary

The government was elected with a bold mandate to modernise Britain and build a fairer, more decent society. To do that and to deliver its key pledges it needs the support of local government. Many councils understand this and are working with local partners to place young people in jobs, raise standards in schools and cut crime. At its best local government is brilliant and cannot be bettered. But to play its full part in modernising Britain local government itself needs to modernise. There are three reasons why change is needed:

- *localities lack a clear sense of direction*: most people have a sense of pride in where they live. They want to see everyone working together to make their town, estate or village a better place to live. But with so many agencies, businesses, groups and organisations now playing a part in local issues, it is often difficult to get everybody working to a common agenda. Localities deserve clearer vision and leadership.

- *there is a lack of coherence and cohesion in delivering local services*: the fragmentation of responsibilities between so many public agencies also affects the services local people receive. Sometimes these agencies work well together as a team. But sometimes co-operation gives way to conflict and local people lose out. And even where the council runs the services, co-ordination between departments often leaves a lot to be desired.

- *the quality of local services is too variable:* the best of the public sector is excellent but too many public bodies are content with the mediocre. And sometimes things are so bad that the government has to intervene.

The answer is not to go back to back to an old model of councils trying to plan and run most services. Instead councils should focus on their role as leaders of local communities by developing a clear vision for their locality, organising and supporting partnerships and guaranteeing quality services for all. However, in order to fulfil this new leadership role councils will need:

- *a new democratic legitimacy*: Britain comes bottom of the European league table for turnout in local elections. And some councils are much better than others in consulting and involving local people. We should consider new ways of making it easier for people to vote, including placing polling booths in shopping malls, holding elections entirely by postal ballot and voting at weekends. Councils should also use surveys, citizens' juries and other methods to make it easier for people to participate in local affairs. Enabling councils to hold referendums could be another way of encouraging this process;

- *new ways of working:* most people do not know the name of the leader of their council. The committee system takes up an enormous amount of time and discourages rather than encourages leadership. A radical overhaul is needed. Councils should separate the executive from the non-executive role of councillors. Directly elected mayors and cabinet-style appointments should be used to develop strong and clear local leadership. Other councillors should have more support in scrutinising decisions, monitoring performance and representing constituents and community groups in their ward;

- *new disciplines*; most councillors and council officers are honest and hardworking. But a tough code of conduct and independent investigation and determination of serious allegations is needed to deal with those few who are corrupt. Councils also have a duty to be efficient and to make sure that residents receive quality services. The government's Best Value framework will help them deliver this, but it will be demanding. And the government will intervene if authorities are incapable of improving their performance;

- *new powers* local authorities will increasingly tackle problems and deliver services in partnership with others. The government is already planning to give councils new partnerships powers on health, services for young children and crime reduction. It will be consulting on whether and how authorities should have more discretion over their finances. And councils that are performing well could be given more freedom and powers to develop new initiatives to address local concerns.

The role of local government has continually changed and evolved over the last 200 years. So the challenge to change again is nothing new. The government wants local authorities to rise to the challenge and work in partnership in building a modern Britain.

Leading the way–
A new vision for local government

The government's mandate

The Labour government was elected with a bold mandate to modernise Britain: to make it a fairer, more decent society. To do this and to deliver our pledges we have to mobilise every level of government.

That means developing policies, establishing priorities, allocating resources, passing legislation and setting targets and timetables. But it also involves changing the means and mechanisms of achieving a modern Britain. A modern country requires modern government. That is why, for example, we are reforming the way that the NHS works so that its structures are geared to raising health standards, breaking down the barriers between health and social care and tackling the causes as well as the effects of ill health. Likewise the introduction of Regional Development Agencies will bring greater coherence and a sharper regional focus to regeneration and economic development. The establishment of an elected mayor as part of a Greater London Authority will provide a powerful vehicle for tackling the many problems that confront the capital. The Scottish Parliament and the Welsh Assembly, by putting power in the hands of the people, will ensure that government policies are more responsive to what people want. And our Better Government project, along with the Comprehensive Spending Review, is examining how government itself can function more effectively to deliver our objectives.

Central government needs modern local government

But however much central government does at the centre it will often be dependent on others to make things happen, on the ground where it matters. And that is where local government comes in. The delivery of the government's key pledges and policies also requires modern local government helping to make change happen. Take Labour's key pledges as an example.

- Our number one priority to raise educational standards needs local authorities to play their part – not by taking back the running of schools or intervening where schools are already doing what they should be, but by setting targets for their areas and working with teachers, governors and parents to help improve those schools that are failing or underperforming.

- The welfare to work programme encourages local authorities to help create and support the partnerships that will identify the posts for the young unemployed to fill, develop child care networks and improve the skills of the workforce in their locality.

- If we are to reduce crime and deal with young offenders we have to improve the way that police and local authorities work with each other and with local communities to design and implement crime reduction strategies.

- The commitment to reduce NHS waiting lists requires better co-ordination between hospital trusts, health authorities and local authorities to stop hospital beds being blocked and to avoid unnecessary admissions.

- Building a sound economy involves local authorities working with businesses, Training and Enterprise Councils (TECs) and chambers of commerce to attract investment and develop strong competitive businesses.

And so the list could go on. Tackling social exclusion, improving public health, implementing Local Agenda 21 on the environment and modernising public transport – progress in all these areas depends on local authorities playing a full and effective part.

In many areas councils already understand this. More and more education authorities are, in partnership with schools, achieving real improvements in literacy: by providing intensive support for children in their first years at school, by strengthening links with parents, and by targeting those pupils with particular problems. The Homecheck service run by Portsmouth council has helped to cut burglaries by providing people aged over 60 with a free home and safety inspection service and by fitting the security devices they need. And in Leeds the council's job placement initiative has shown how a tailored programme can overcome the barriers to work such as a lack of skills, childcare difficulties, limited experience and low self-esteem, and find people jobs. Supported by the local hospital, TEC, a partnership of major employers and 1,250 small and medium-sized companies, the Leeds programme has placed 350 unemployed people in training and 975 in supported jobs. 250 lone parents have come off benefit and returned to work.

Many other councils can boast similar records of achievement in helping to drive and shape change. Local government at its best is brilliant and cannot be bettered. That is why one of our first acts was to establish a Central Local partnership, chaired by the Deputy Prime Minister: a forum where Ministers and councillors can discuss how best to support local diversity and innovation and harness local government's capacity to deliver the government's modern agenda.

New role with old roots

Helping with modernisation is, in many ways, not a new role for local authorities. Local government's *raison d'etre* has always been as the engine of modernisation and innovation.

When in the early part of the last century, government found that it could not cope with the effects of the growing industrialisation and urbanisation it looked to local solutions or, in some cases, had local solutions thrust upon it. It was for that reason that central government breathed life into ancient city corporations, set up new elected boards and established municipal and county councils to help forge a modern society.

It was the councillors, board members and aldermen of former generations that transformed public health through the provision of sewers and clean water, made possible universal education, built and maintained the great arterial roads, developed public transport, bought decent and affordable housing within the reach of millions, provided public parks, baths and libraries and organised care and welfare for the elderly and those in need.

When the post-war Labour government decided to introduce modern town planning, it was local councils that were given the task of making the system work. It was local authorities that were asked to bear the brunt of building the homes in the wake of bomb damage and a chronic housing shortage. And it was local education authorities that provided the classrooms and appointed the teachers when school numbers increased and when the school leaving age was raised first to 15 and then 16.

Local government has to change if it is to be part of the modernisation project

But for local government to play its part fully in helping to create a modern society as we enter a new millennium, local government itself needs to change.

That also is not anything new for local government. Local government's role has constantly changed and evolved. For nearly 200 years local authorities have been developing, gaining and shedding services. Sometimes the changes have been top-down. As central government first assumed responsibilities for services such as education or, in more recent times, food safety, it used local authorities to deliver them. Sometimes, as services developed and circumstances changed, government has moved functions away from local government to another agency. Health services and social security, for example, became national responsibilities.

However, a lot of change has been generated not by central government but by bottom-up initiative. Local authorities elected by local people have a proud record of responding to the needs of their communities and pioneering new services, from gas, electricity and telephones to airports and community alarms – services which other agencies and sectors have then picked up and developed.

That spirit of innovation still lives. Despite the previous government's actions to undermine and belittle local government, the last 20 years has seen councils developing new roles on economic development and inward investment, the environment, child care and crime prevention.

So local government's own history and experience prepares it for the need to change again if it is to play its full part in modernising Britain as we move into the next century.

There has to be change because we cannot leave things as they are. The current position is not sustainable. It is getting in the way of the government achieving its objectives.

There are three main challenges

Localities lack a clear sense of direction

Leadership and strong government are qualities that are needed as much at local level as at national level. Most people have a sense of pride in where they live. They want to see everyone working together to make their town, estate or village a better place to live. But the Conservatives deliberately sought to diffuse and dilute power in each locality. Not all their initiatives were bad but the overall legacy is a damaging fragmentation of powers and responsibilities. Localities deserve clearer vision and leadership. If local people are to enjoy a sound economy and a better quality of life and if communities are to deal with difficult cross-cutting issues like youth justice, drug abuse and social exclusion, we have to harness the contribution of businesses, public agencies, voluntary organisations and community groups and get them working to a common agenda.

A lack of coherence and cohesion in delivering local services

The fragmentation of responsibilities is also affecting the services local people receive. There are all sorts of players on the local pitch jostling for position where previously the council was the main game in town – TECs, Child Protection Committees, Health Authorities, NHS Trusts, Grant Maintained Schools, Further Education Colleges, Police Liaison Committees, Police Authorities, Fire Authorities, Single Regeneration Budget Partnerships, Probation Committees, Drug Action Teams, Magistrates Courts Committees, Development Agencies, Joint Planning Committees and Joint Consultative Committees.

Sometimes they work well together as a team. But sometimes someone takes their bat home with the result that co-operation gives way to conflict and local people lose out. Time and again inquiries into child abuse cases have identified a breakdown in communication between agencies as a major factor in what went wrong. The Audit Commission report on the youth justice system highlighted the need to improve the co-ordination between the various agencies involved with young people in trouble. And it is difficult for the public to know whom to hold to account for what. For example, if beds in the local hospital are blocked, do local people blame the hospital trust for trying to dump the problem on the council or should they criticise the social services department for failing to work properly with the local health authority? Or are both to blame? The partnership-working needed to guarantee reliable local services is too much of a hit and miss affair.

The quality of local services is too variable

The best of the public sector is excellent but too many public bodies are content with the mediocre. And as the evidence of the Audit Commission, OFSTED and the Social Services Inspectorate inspections show, there are just too many councils failing to deliver acceptable standards of service to their citizens. Failure of this sort, whatever its cause, cannot be tolerated. It may not only blight the chance of a child receiving a decent education but affect his or her opportunities throughout life. And at its worst such failure can result in harm for elderly people and abuse of children.

In many ways the situation is akin to that existing over 100 years ago when there was a patchwork quilt of boards, boroughs, committees and councils that were providing services in a fragmented, overlapping and incoherent way. The answer then was the great municipal reform Acts which rationalised the duties, functions and powers of local authorities.

Those reforms stood the test of time. They paved the way for the multi-purpose local authority as we know it. A model which reached its zenith in the post 1945 settlement and the expansion of the welfare state in the 1960s and early 1970s, with authorities responsible for planning and delivering an ever-growing range of services.

But the answer to today's problems cannot be to go back to the local government model of a bygone age. We all need to learn from the past. And just as there were many successes, there were many failures:

- a failure to explain, particularly when it came to explaining the reason for the council's budget decisions;

- a failure to engage the participation of local citizens, particularly council tenants for whom the council was – and often still is – an unresponsive, even incompetent landlord;

- a failure too often, to work in partnership with local companies and voluntary bodies, in favour of a universal 'council knows best and can do everything' approach to the provision of local services; and

- a failure to put the needs of service users ahead of those of service providers.

The solution, therefore, does not lie in local authorities gathering again unto themselves all the functions and roles they once had. Not only would it mean more costly and time-consuming upheaval but a flawed model is not the answer to today's problems.

For example, poor co-ordination between agencies would not be solved by putting services back under the local authority umbrella. Many local authorities have not yet achieved effective co-ordination between services for which they already do have responsibility. Tensions between social services, housing and education are still too common. And there is many an MP who knows about the tenant being threatened with eviction for arrears when the real problem is mistakes and confusion over the housing benefit entitlement.

Nor does local authority control automatically solve the problem of weak accountability. Participation in local elections is poor. Britain is at the bottom of the European league table for turnout in local government elections. And in many areas the trust in local government is not as strong as it needs to be.

And the variable quality of services will not necessarily improve by making councils responsible for them. In some areas local authorities may match or better the performance of other agencies but in others their record is worse.

So the new local government must move on from where we are. But it cannot go back. It must, therefore, be based on a new third way.

The new local government – a third way

We need a new – a different – local government to continue the task of modernising Britain. A new role for a new millennium. A role that challenges the sense of inevitable decline that has hung over local government for the past 20 years and provides local people and their representatives with new opportunities.

At the heart of local government's new role is leadership – leadership that gives vision, partnership and quality of life to cities, towns and villages all over Britain. It will mean councils using their unique status and authority as directly elected bodies to:

Develop a vision for their locality. Working with other interests, agencies and groups they will develop a shared view of what needs to be done for the well-being of their area. By being in touch with local concerns and needs they will build community support for an agenda that may range from tackling social and economic decline, to building a new tram system, to tackling drug abuse, to improving education and training standards, to protecting the environment, to developing centres of excellence for the arts and recreation, to revitalising town centres.

Provide a focus for partnership. The days of the all-purpose authority that planned and delivered everything are gone. They are finished. It is in partnership with others – public agencies, private companies, community groups and voluntary organisations – that local government's future lies. Local authorities will still deliver some services but their distinctive leadership role will be to weave and knit together the contribution of the various local stakeholders. To ensure that the shared vision is delivered by bringing cohesion and co-ordination to the current fragmented scene. They will mobilise investment, bid for funds, champion the needs of the area and harness the energies of local people and community organisations. Councils will no longer be defined just by lists of statutory responsibilities but by what, in partnership with others, they achieve.

Guarantee quality services for all. The new local government will bring pride back to towns and cities by ensuring that the streets are clean and safe, the grass cut and the parks maintained. It will build trust in local councils by making sure the schools are good, homes repaired and that vulnerable children and the frail elderly are properly cared for. The new local government will lead by example and listen and involve local citizens in planning and reviewing services. It will set targets, monitor performance and take prompt and effective action as soon as things start to go wrong. The new local government will use its leadership role to facilitate and enable other agencies and organisations operating in its area to account for their decisions to local people.

Many councils are already pursuing parts of this agenda. They are working with local organisations and businesses to map out the future priorities and plans for their locality. They are key players in the SRB partnerships that have brought jobs, homes and security to areas that had been written off. They have formed partnerships with health authorities and others to develop healthy cities. They are concentrating less on running estates and more on working with developers and housing associations to identify and meet local housing needs. They have reorganised departments to meet the special needs of particular groups, such as children or elderly people. They have led the way in developing one-stop shops and information help-lines to make it easier for people to use services.

But if local government is to be effective in this new role then it has to re-think every aspect of how it functions. It has to deal with obstacles that are undermining its claim to exercise local leadership.

New local government requires new legitimacy

Local government's credentials to be community leaders are weakened by its poor base of popular support. Turn-out for local elections is around 40% and 25% in many inner city councils – the very authorities which most need to mobilise their communities behind bold initiatives to tackle local problems. In a recent by-election in Liverpool, the turnout was just 6% in a result that affected the political control of the council. That kind of thing makes a mockery of democracy.

It may be asking too much to expect local government to get people shouting from the rooftops. But it is not too much to expect most people to care enough to vote or to know who to praise or blame for what is going on in their locality.

Revitalising local democracy is a big task. We in the political parties have a duty to recruit first rate councillors and to take local campaigning seriously. I see this as a high priority for Labour. And that is why we have set up Project 99 to attract, select and train the best candidates from all walks of life for the local elections in 1999.

However, it is not just a matter of action for political parties. We need to get local government's internal structures right – particularly its structures for accountability and leadership – without which councils will never properly mobilise their electorates.

The government has set up a Working Party under Home Office Minister, George Howarth, to examine how we can increase the number of people registered to vote and how to make voting easier. The government will shortly be publishing a Consultation Paper on how it might modernise the electoral system – including the possibility of conducting local elections entirely by postal ballot, voting at weekends and having polling stations at supermarkets and shopping centres.

But it is not just representative democracy that needs to be strengthened. We also need to look at other democratic initiatives that will strengthen community leadership. Councils need to avoid getting trapped in the secret world of the caucus and the party group. They should let local people have their say. Some authorities are doing this. Citizens' juries are helping to build consensus for tackling difficult issues. Local surveys are being used more and more to identify local concerns. And the local referendum could become part and parcel of a council's tool kit to help it exercise its leadership function.

Every authority should set itself targets for improving voter turnout and strengthening local participation in the government of their community.

New local government requires new ways of working

The way that local government currently operates is inefficient and opaque. It is not fit for its modern role. Councillors are very diligent and spend many hours on civic business. But, as the Audit Commission reported last year, 'too much of a burden is placed on councillors, often unproductively, by committee meetings'. Sitting on all these committees puts people off entering local politics. And it's not where the real discussions take place. In most councils it is the political groups which make the big and significant decisions.

But the heart of the problem is that local government needs recognised leaders if it is to fulfil the community leadership role. Committees have their place but as a way providing community leadership they are weak vessels. People and outside organisations need to know who is politically responsible for running the council. How many people know the leader of their authority – or just as important, the chair of the education committee? And why don't they know them? Because local people have no direct say over their local leaders. And because the shifting sands of committee membership and chairs fails to foster leaders and leadership. Executive leadership needs to be visible. An individual can provide a clear focus for local leadership as experience in France, Germany, New Zealand, Canada and the United States show.

In short, we need to separate the executive from the representative role. Both have a part an important part to play in community leadership but in different and complementary ways. At present, the law does not allow for direct leadership models.

That is why we are giving Londoners a referendum on having an elected mayor. And the Bill sponsored by Lord Hunt will allow the concept to be piloted in other areas. The leaders of our major towns and cities deserve to be big players on the national stage – influential figures in their own right, as they are in other countries. If they used the provisions in Lord Hunt's Bill to elect their leaders directly they would demonstrably have the people's support and the democratic legitimacy to play that role.

Of course, elected mayors are not the only way of enhancing leadership. Lord Hunt's Bill also allows councils to experiment with other forms of executive government. Cabinet government at local level, for example.

A focus on a strong executive does not mean that the role of the backbencher is unimportant. On the contrary the job of the non-executive councillor is vital. Executives need to be held to account – even if at times that process can be frustrating and painful! Constituents have problems that need resolving. And local groups and residents need help and support. I want to see non-executive councillors spending more time in their communities and less in committees. Many councillors are already acting as community leaders of their ward and there is great scope to develop this role.

Separating the executive from the representative function could help the political parties with the task of attracting more people back into local government. At present local councillors as a whole are not as representative as they could be of the communities they serve. Nearly half of councillors are over 55 – 35% are retired – and just one in 10 is under 40. Only a quarter are women. And ethnic minorities are also under-represented. Making the executive distinct, separate and fairly rewarded and supported will help to attract more people of calibre into leadership positions. And making scrutiny the prime backbench function will cut the inordinate number of hours spent deliberating on committees. So local people who want contribute to their local community by standing for public office will know that they can do so without signing half their life away.

Every single authority should examine how they function and decide how best they should structure their council around the new leadership role.

The new ways of working should also involve council officers as well as council members. Senior managers must provide clear vision and leadership to their staff. They need to challenge and break down those professional and departmental barriers that hold back innovation and modernisation. They must engage with the leaders of the local community – both inside and outside the council. And, most crucial of all, they must not get so remote from the front line that they get out of touch with the day-to-day service that ordinary people experience.

Central and local government should also improve the way they work together. In staffing the Social Exclusion Unit we have drawn on local government experience and expertise. But why is this such a rare occurrence? Why should not the best head teachers, directors of education and social care spend some time working in the appropriate department helping government to develop policy? And why cannot we have more civil servants spending time working for local authorities and local partnerships? Might there be a case for a common public sector career path between town hall and Whitehall?

And there are other ways that central and local government can combine to change the way they both work to improve services for local people. For example, wouldn't it make sense for government and council benefit offices to pilot ways of administering benefits jointly? And what about councils using their leadership role to set up 24-hour information lines – not just for their own services but for all the government and public agencies in their area? I know that the Local Government Association is working with government Ministers on ideas like this through the Central-Local Partnership. We are also committed to breaking down the organisational and financial barriers between councils and other agencies to make it easier to deliver seamless and integrated services to local citizens. We are, for example, examining ways that health authorities and local authorities could be given greater flexibility to operate pooled budgets to fund services which cut across the health/social care divide.

New local government requires new disciplines

Local authorities will only be able to exercise a leadership role in their communities if they command respect from their citizens and support from their partners. Councillors and officials that are incompetent or corrupt not only undermine their leadership credentials but sully the reputation of local government as a whole. We cannot and will not tolerate corruption and malpractice.

The government will be publishing proposals, based on Lord Nolan's report on local government conduct, for a new framework of standards for all local authorities. It will require every council to adopt its own code of conduct based on a nationally approved model. And it will also need to include provision for swift and independent investigation and determination of all serious allegations of malpractice.

The vast majority of councillors are decent, honest and incredibly hard working. We cannot let the behaviour of a few undermine the reputation of the many.

For leadership to be effective authorities also have to show that they can use the powers and resources at their disposal efficiently and effectively. The more that authorities demonstrate that they are delivering Best Value the stronger their credentials for leading local partnerships.

Best value will mean councils being clear about their priorities and objectives, reviewing a proportion of their services each year, examining every single aspect of a service's performance and making year-on-year improvements. And the local auditor will want to be satisfied that councils are not taking any short cuts at any stage. At the heart of the Best Value process will be four tools – the four Cs – which councils will use to make sure their services are of the highest qualities:

- *challenging* the underlying purpose, objectives, structures and costs of a service;

- *consulting* with those who use services to make sure that they are responsive to their needs and concerns, and with those who provide them to tap their ideas for increasing the efficiency and quality of services;

- *comparing* the performance of services with others, using performance indicators and benchmarking to see how improvements can be made; and

- *competing* with other providers to make sure that services are provided in the most cost-efficient way possible.

This is a demanding process. But if local people are to receive quality services on a consistent basis, then it has to be this way. Best Value is not a short cut for getting out of compulsory competitive tendering. Nor does it does not mean councils going soft on competition and just going back to automatically delivering services themselves. The new local government will mean councils doing less but being involved in more spheres of activity. But the competition must be fair – fair to Council Tax payers and fair to employees. Cost counts, but so does quality. Where councils can show that they can provide best value by delivering quality services in a cost-effective and competitive manner in-house, then it will make sense for them to do so – but only if they meet those conditions. Increasingly the pattern will be for authorities to enter into more partnerships and joint ventures with businesses and voluntary agencies and other public bodies to deliver local services.

Those authorities that persistently fail Best Value standards for any of their services will not only forfeit their role as community leaders, they will ultimately forfeit the right to be responsible for services they cannot manage effectively. The government will not hesitate to intervene directly to secure improvements where services fall below acceptable standards. And, if necessary, it will look to other authorities and agencies to take on duties where an authority is manifestly incapable of providing an effective service and unwilling to take the action necessary to improve its performance.

But the more local authorities embrace Best Value the more they will point the way for the others to follow. Local government has the opportunity to shape the future agenda for public sector efficiency, economy and effectiveness. I am encouraged that 150 councils in England and others in Scotland and Wales applied to pilot Best Value. That is a good start. And those councils which have not yet got round to thinking about what Best Value means for their authority need to get on with it if they are not to find themselves left behind and struggling to catch up.

New local government requires new powers

Where councils embrace this agenda of change and show that they can adapt to play a part in modernising their locality, then they will find their status and powers enhanced.

Already the Government is legislating for authorities to have a key role in drawing up the Early Years Development Plans in partnership with the voluntary and private sectors. We are also promoting the new local government role in the way that our crime reduction strategy is being framed and the way that the NHS is to be modernised. Local authorities will share a statutory duty of partnership with police authorities to work on reducing crime. Councils will form an integral part of Health Improvement Programmes which will focus action to improve public health and shape the delivery of health care in each locality.

The Bill sponsored by Lord Hunt which the Government is supporting provides new opportunities to develop community leadership. We shall be consulting on whether and how authorities should have greater discretion over the setting of business rates and over how the government might implement a new duty on councils to promote the economic, social and environmental well-being of their area.

But increased rights require increased responsibility. If the government is to increase local authorities' capacity to act it will expect evidence of local authorities modernising themselves in order to take on new responsibilities. There is little point in giving extra powers and functions to authorities that are not dealing adequately with the responsibilities they currently have. But equally there is no reason why those councils which are performing well should be held back by those who are not.

One possibility for reforming the capital allocation system would be, as with the current system for housing finance, to partly relate an authority's ability to invest to how well it uses its existing assets and has prepared its capital programme. And one option for a more general power of community initiative would be to make it dependent on councils demonstrating that they have adopted modern leadership structures and that they enjoy broad community support.

If you change we'll reward

I want the message to local government to be loud and clear.

A changing role is part of your heritage. The people's needs require you to change again so that you can play your part in helping to modernise Britain and, in partnership with others, deliver the policies on which this government was elected.

If you accept this challenge, you will not find us wanting. You can look forward to an enhanced role and new powers. Your contribution will be recognised. Your status enhanced.

If you are unwilling or unable to work to the modern agenda then the government will have to look to other partners to take on your role.

The choice for local government is clear. I hope that councils all over the land will choose to work with a modern government for a modern Britain.